The 90% Wealth Solution

Building Wealth through Real Estate Investing

by Jayson Morris

"90% of all millionaires become so through owning real estate."

Andrew Carnegie

Table of Contents

Introduction

I would like to thank you for purchasing "The 90% Wealth Solution."

Real estate investing is perhaps the oldest and the most popular form of investing. For all those who have been searching for information about real estate investing, there are multiple forums, blogs, books and videos on the Internet on this subject. However, all of this information can prove to be quite overwhelming for someone who is just getting started with real estate investing.

Up until now, one has had to search on the Internet to gain a basic understanding of real estate investing. Well, things are about to change and your search ends right here.

In this book, you will find all the information you need to get started with real estate investing. You will learn such things as the basics of real estate investing, its benefits, the manner in which you can bounce back from any bad experiences in the past, creating the right mental attitude for investing, taking the necessary steps for getting started, and not letting certain setbacks hold you back. Real estate investing can be quite profitable when done right and this book will help you in this process.

So, without any further ado, let's get started!

Chapter 1: Getting Started With Real Estate Investing

One of the most popular forms of investing is real estate investing. By adding real estate investing to your investment portfolio, you are not only adding the necessary diversification but are also protecting your wealth from the extremely volatile stock market. Regardless of whether you are investing in real estate for the first time or are already involved in real estate investing, here are a few general steps for getting started.

You will need to determine the amount of time and money that you are willing to spend on an investment. You should always set your budget; it helps in planning things out. Always do your research, find out the different options that are available to you. Select an investment that will fit your financial requirements.

For instance, REIT investing requires relatively less time and money whereas you will need more funds for direct real estate investing. You will need to save up cash for all the investment related expenses that can crop up without prior notice. An investor interested in direct real estate investment will need to have a bigger cash cushion than other investors. You should always be prepared for setbacks. As with any other investing avenue, setbacks are quite common. You will need to be prepared to face these challenges. You will learn more about all these things in the upcoming chapters.

There are different types of real estate investments and knowing about these different options will help you in making an informed decision. Several types of real estate investments are mentioned below.

Rental properties

For becoming a direct owner on the real estate market, you will need to find a property (home, apartment or a condo), buy it, and then rent it out to tenants. Before you become a landlord, there are a few things that you will need to do. You will need funds for a down payment, a property inspection, and a review of the potential rental revenue from the property as well as the likely expenses.

There are various benefits that this form of investment offers. You can expect a steady cash flow as well as an opportunity for capital appreciation along with several other tax benefits. However, you will need to do the necessary due diligence before zeroing in on a rental property. You can hire the services of a real estate agent who deals with investment properties and start touring some that have potential to be high performing assets. Be prepared to do the necessary homework for evaluating the financial health of a property. You will need to make sure that the investment will indeed provide you with a good return.

Real estate investment trusts

These are popularly referred to as REITs. This category of real estate investment includes companies that hold or finances real estate that generates an income. REITs acquire multiple properties that could include apartment buildings, office buildings, hotels, hospitals, industrial units and even mortgages. These companies then sell these assets as ownership shares to other investors.

The benefits that a REIT investor would enjoy are the same as the ones that a direct real estate investor would enjoy. A REIT will need to pay out at least 90% of the taxable income it earns to its shareholders on a yearly basis. REITs are a good hedge against inflation in the market. These funds can increase in value. However, there is no guarantee of positive returns. If you are making a purchase during a housing boom, when the prices return to the normal level, the value of the REIT that you are holding will likely drop. Investing in REITs is as easy as investing in a mutual fund or exchange-traded fund.

Real estate investment groups

For starting a real estate investment group, you will need to pool your funds with the funds of other investors and then acquire a property along with them. You get to enjoy all the benefits of holding a rental property without having to worry about the accompanying responsibilities of cash and management of the property. By joining a real estate investment group, you will get an opportunity to learn about real estate investing as well as get the experience of investing in real estate. However, on the downside, it isn't that easy to work with others and at times it does get complicated. There may also be special legal considerations for participating or starting a real estate investment group. Therefore, be sure that you have thoroughly read and have understood the various policies of the group before you join one. Always have an exit strategy in mind, in case things go south.

Short term rentals

With the introduction of the concept of the sharing economy and various websites like Airbnb, even an ordinary individual can become a landlord. You will need to, however, understand the reasons for which you would want to become a rental host. You will need to make a serious commitment, have a financial strategy, take out necessary insurance and think about management if you are interested in renting out your property by making use of the sharing economy. There are multiple benefits of renting out a part of your home. You can enjoy some extra cash flow, meet new people, and earn income from that part of your property that isn't being used at the moment. You will need to prepare a website for visitors, manage the listings and always be available for answering any questions the potential guest might have, manage the property and keep it clean.

Regardless of the investing route that you choose, you will need to evaluate your own reasons for investing and the circumstances in which you are investing. If you want, you can even start out slowly by making a small investment in a REIT since it is an affordable option when compared to buying an apartment building.

Chapter 2: Why Real Estate Investing is Worth the Effort

Real estate investing might not be for everyone. It does take a lot of motivation and a willingness to keep up with the current market trends. You will also need to be willing to take a few calculated risks. However, real estate investing offers a lot of benefits, such as generating passive income and leaving a family legacy. So, let us take a look at why investing in real estate is definitely worth your while.

Creating long-term wealth

Real estate is one of the best, most battle tested ways to create long-term wealth. For instance, let us assume that you have purchased a farm and started to work on that farm and it's your family business. Over a period of time, the mortgage on that farm would be paid off and, eventually, you would own that piece of land free and clear. Obviously, it is easier to run a farm when you don't have to worry about the burden of a mortgage looming over your head.

The property would definitely be a good investment and it made your family business possible. This is slightly different than your regular "buy and hold" form of real estate investing. However, the end result is the same - holding a property that is free from all loan burdens. If you acquire a property today, then after a period of 30 years or so, the property would be free of all encumbrances. If you can find a way of obtaining positive cash flow from this property, then your tenants are essentially buying this property for you over the years. This is the beauty of investing in real estate.

Take it slow, if you want to

If you are hesitant about becoming a full-time real estate investor, then there are different options that are available to you. Anyone can buy a rental property. This investment can also be passed along to future generations. What if you purchase a new rental property, every ten years of your working life and then passed this portfolio on to the next generation? Even this small portfolio, will end up creating a nice family legacy and create a base of wealth for the future generations. As mentioned earlier, even a little bit of real estate can definitely go a long way if you desire to build a family fortune. This long-term asset is quite sustainable and it does make a great base for building wealth in the long run.

Generating cash flow

In any traditional business, it will take you a few years before your business is throwing off a positive cash flow. However, this isn't necessarily the case with real estate investments. If done properly, your real estate investment should earn you a positive cash flow quite soon after the initial investment.

In many real estate markets, especially in the Midwest, the monthly rent you earn from the property will outweigh the cost of the long-term, fixed rate mortgage. Even after deducting all the expenses incurred on the property, you will be able to start earning as soon as you find a tenant for your property. Over a period of time, your profit margin will also improve when you gradually increase your monthly rent, while your mortgage payments will stay the same. You can start earning passive income from a modest investment in a down payment. At a most basic level, all you have to do is invest in a quality property, find a responsible tenant, manage the property and the tenant and let your investment do the rest of the work for you.

Several tax deductions

The federal government offers several tax benefits for encouraging investment in real estate. There are several deductions that you can make use of as well and this will improve your overall return on investment (ROI). The expenses that you incur for maintaining the rental property are deductible from the income you earn from the property. Even the amount of depreciation on the value of the property is deductible. The income from a rental property is also taxed at a lower rate than the income from any regular business and you needn't necessarily pay self-employment tax either. Not just this, when you sell your real estate investment, the gains from it are taxed at a much lower rate than the gain from capital income, instead of the regular taxation rates of income.

Tax savings

If you are investing in real estate as a part of your retirement plan, then there are several ways in which you can save on taxes. The IRS allows for real estate investments through self-directed IRAs. However, there are certain terms and conditions applicable on this and you should be aware of these. One of the main benefits of investing in real estate in an IRA is that you could defer the payment of taxes as long as you keep these gains (including the income from rental property as well as any profits on sale) in your IRA.

Appreciation in the long run

Real estate investments will help you in creating a steady long-term return. Even with all the fluctuations in the marketplace, the value of real estate tends to increase at a faster pace than inflation over the long run. As the population keeps growing, the need for housing grows with it and this pushes up the market prices of real estate investments. In the long run, the returns from this form of investment can be compared to the stock market, but that is before taking into account the additional savings on tax that real estate offers.

Control

The yields on stock market investments and real estate investments might be quite similar. However, the degree of control offered by the latter is quite high. When you are investing in the stock of a company, you have hardly any control over the decisions of the company that would affect your investment. With real estate, you can do plenty of research and select the most profitable of investments, increase the value of the property by renovating it, and also set the rental rate as you see fit. While taking care of rental properties does require a lot of work, the profits that you reap from it are considerably higher than regular stock market investments.

Debt leverage

Being able to leverage debt is an important strategy for the growth of your real estate investment portfolio. This is because debt allows you to earn a profit by making use of someone else's money. In the case of real estate investment, this "someone else" would be the mortgage lender who is financing the property. If you have rented out this property for the duration of the mortgage, then you will be able to successfully pay off the debt you have incurred on the purchase of the property by making use of the rental income you receive. Eventually, the debt on the property will be paid off and you will have only paid a fraction of the whole sum from your own earnings.

Positive impact on the community

Real estate investing also has the potential of having a positive impact on the community, by making improvements to the property in your area and by providing good housing options for the residents in a given area. More often than not, people tend to rent properties from owners who don't take much pride in maintaining the property. By being a landlord of good repute, you can feel good that you are contributing to the betterment of society while earning a good profit for yourself.

There aren't many investment strategies out there that will offer you all the benefits that real estate investing does.

Chapter 3: Try Again

You might have experienced certain setbacks when you got started with real estate investing. In this chapter, we will take a look at certain things that you should do and those things you should avoid to alleviate the potency of any setbacks.

Coming back from foreclosures and short sales

In the last decade, foreclosures and short sales have been prevalent. However, there are certain things that you can do to make sure that you don't have to go through this again.

Be aware of your options

You don't have to wait for a period of seven years after a foreclosure before buying another property. The original period you had to wait for buying a new property after a foreclosure sale (short sale) and a foreclosure changed from four and seven years to two and three years respectively. The standard period of waiting is three years for getting a loan from the Federal Housing Administration. It could also be just one year depending on the circumstances.

Changing your habits

You will need to change your spending habits. You should focus on repaying any debt, creating a viable savings strategy, and avoid splurging on any new purchases. One of the biggest obstacles that investors face is saving funds for a down payment and closing costs. One way to overcome this challenge is to start saving up all of your bonuses, any windfall gains, refunds on tax returns and any other related savings in your savings account. You can also build your reserve for down payments by setting up an automatic deposit link to your savings account. This will help you in getting rid of any unnecessary temptations for spending your money.

Repairing your credit

In most cases, the necessary credit score that you need to obtain financing backed by the FHA is 580. However, many of the mortgage lenders require a minimum FICO (credit score that is created by Fair Isaac Corporation) score of 640. You can build up your credit score by paying off any high-interest debts you might have and by not taking out any additional loans. If you can report your timely repayments to any of the big credit bureaus, your credit score will improve.

Seeking professional help

You can always seek help from professionals in this field who will help you with the whole investing process. They may be able to help you manage your credit issues and also come up with strategies for stimulating savings.

Overcoming bad experiences owning rental property

Now, let us take a look at certain things that will help ensure that you limit any bad experiences with owning rental property.

Have reasonable expectations

Your goal for real estate investing should be to maintain a positive cash flow. However, you shouldn't have unrealistic expectations like acquiring a yacht at the end of the year. If you have your expectations in check, then you will be able to resist the temptation of unnecessarily increasing the rent or of driving out good tenants. Also, by having reasonable expectations, you will be less likely to take risks that might lead to huge losses.

Earning and effort

Do you want to take the hands-on approach or do you want to work with a property manager? Theoretically, you can increase your earnings by self-managing your properties. If your current cash flow is tight, then you might think twice about hiring a property manager. However, it isn't just that simple. There is a saying "Don't be penny wise and pound foolish." A good property manager could be worth her weight in gold.

Rules matter

There are different federal and state laws that would provide you with an outline for understanding all your responsibilities as well as liabilities. Spend some time on research so that you understand the different rules that you need to be aware of.

Get the property inspected

If you are interested in avoiding any unexpected expenses, then it is prudent that you get the property inspected by a third party professional before you make a buying decision. This has saved me from buying a bad property. Ask around for references of good home inspectors. Yes, it is another expense but the cost of a good home inspection could end up saving you thousands of dollars in the long run.

References and credit checks

Many landlords rush to fill vacancies in an effort to keep the cash flowing. There is nothing wrong with wanting to keep your cash flow steady. However, rushing to fill a vacancy with any warm body could actually lead to huge losses. Take your time and find a good, responsible tenant. It is better to let the property be empty for a while than accept a tenant who might not keep paying rent or who might trash the property. After all, it is your property and you will need to make sure that the tenant's references and credit worthiness hold good in order to protect your investment.

Association of Landlords

If you decide to self-manage your properties, consider joining the local landlord's association as this will provide you with a brain trust that you can tap when questions arise. You can obtain samples of leases, learn about the local laws and regulations, and also obtain a list of lawyers, contractors and inspectors. You will need to have a lawyer, a tax professional and a banker on board if you want to own and manage property on your own. They will not only help you in avoiding any potential pitfalls but will also guide you when you get put in a sticky situation.

Insurance matters

You will need to buy the right kind of insurance once you are aware of all the rules and regulations. This will help you in securing your property against any potential damages. Look into what insurance your tenants should have as well.

Always have an emergency fund

Expenses can come up without prior notice. Therefore, it is important that you have a fund for such unexpected expenditures. A basic rule of thumb in this regard is to set aside a fund that amounts to about 20% of the value of the property you own. You can build this fund by saving a portion of the rental revenue every month in a maintenance account.

Overcoming the experience of managing bad tenants

Friendly but firm

You certainly won't be able to lease many properties by being a cold and controlling property manager. While you are leasing out your property, make sure that you are very clear about the terms of the lease. Be clear about what you expect from the tenants, terms of payment, the upkeep of the property, guests, about pets and so on. Be firm when you are explaining the rules of engagement to your tenant if you want to avoid any unnecessary unpleasantness in the future. Don't let the tenant take undue advantage of your friendly nature. You need to be clear about the basic rules of the tenancy; and this doesn't mean that you shouldn't be friends with your tenant.

A good property manager will make the tenant feel welcome and will be helpful to them as well. However, showing too much solidarity with the tenant can often lead to them testing the limits of this relationship. You should be friendly, understanding, helpful, but firm at the same time. Staying strong could be mildly awkward if the person collecting the late fee or making the demand is the same one the tenant contacts as a general rule. If you want, you could always make someone else be the "enforcer." Regardless of what you decide to do, you will need to be upfront about the conditions of the tenancy and not hesitate in putting your foot down on certain matters. For instance, if there is a no-pets policy in the apartment complex, then allowing your tenant to have a pet wouldn't be fair to the other residents.

A written agreement

You should always have a comprehensive lease

agreement. A regular standardized lease form would be helpful, but it wouldn't include all of the specific policies that you may want to enforce, or they wouldn't take into account all the specific features, amenities, or special needs of the particular property that you are leasing out. Take some time and customize the lease agreement by taking into consideration all the different things that are different from a standard lease agreement and any rules or different expectations that are specific to the property being rented out.

Important notices

Every property owner will have faced a situation in which the renter would claim that they haven't received the notice about an important matter, or for delaying the action that was demanded to be taken. This can be avoided by making use of certified mail for all important notices. This will help in ensuring that the said notice was sent by including the mail number, sending a second copy of the same through regular mail, and by keeping one copy of the notice yourself as well. You should keep a stack of all the certified mail postcards and receipt slips before going to the post office. By doing this, you can successfully get rid of the "I never got the mail/notice" excuse and save yourself a world of pain.

Preparing in advance

If you happen to be lucky, then you won't find yourself stuck in any legal issues with your renters. The laws governing renter's protection are quite arcane and there are those who find loopholes in these laws and end up troubling unaware property managers. This is the reason why you need to be familiar with these different laws or have an attorney on hand whenever some trouble crops up. You should always make a note of any lease violations, complaints from neighbors, and the problems experienced so that in case any legal trouble ensues, you have got all the necessary evidence.

Considering the neighborhood

Most neighborhoods tend to have homeowner's associations, neighborhood watches and several other formal and informal organizations. These can have several rules or expectations regarding the parking of vehicles, pets in the parks, garbage pickup rules, and so on. If you want to be a good property manager, you can avoid a lot of problems by simply being aware of these rules and intimating the same to the potential tenants before they move in.

Moving-out trouble

A savvy property owner will include an "intention to vacate" notice and clause in every lease agreement and review the same with the renter. If you have been renting out your property for a while, then you might have had some trouble with a renter who may fail to give a notice or perhaps a renter asked you to adjust the amount from their security deposit as the last month's rent. A security deposit and rent are two different things, and it is referred to as a security deposit for a reason and it stays important to have one until the day the tenant actually moves out.

The notice period will allow the owner to find a new tenant so that the property doesn't stay empty when the current tenant moves out. If you feel like it, you can explain these things to the potential tenants and also state that if the rent is left unpaid, then it will affect their credit. You need to be firm about these things from the get go if you want to minimize unnecessary conflicts, tensions and misunderstandings in the future at the time of moving out.

Get an attorney if necessary

If it becomes necessary to evict a tenant, you will need an attorney. Don't just randomly choose an attorney. You can ask others for references and inquire if the attorney deals with eviction matters and property issues. Always do some research before contacting an attorney and vet the attorney by asking them a few necessary questions. You should ask them if they have ever been involved in eviction matters, the number of evictions that they undertake in a month, and the time it takes for them to get one done. You can also ask them about the amount of time it would take for getting the case before a judge and so on. This will help you in understanding whether or not the particular attorney is cut out for your case.

Regardless of how careful you have been, you will

eventually run into some problem or other with your renters. Therefore, make sure that you have made things clear from the first day and stick to your policies. This will make life much easier for you. Also, you needn't feel guilty if you haven't been able to accommodate any special consideration that your renter has asked of you.

You need to remember that you are running a business and it isn't a charity. If the renter says that he isn't able to pay the rent or it'll take a few more weeks to pay the rent due, then in such a case, you needn't feel bad, unless the problem is genuine and important. Remember, you should be friendly but firm as well.

I have spent a lot of time in this chapter on the basics of good property management. There is a good reason for this. Property management can make or break your investment. I believe property management is a bigger factor than the location of your investment or the specific amenities of your investment. This why I stated that a good property manager is worth her weight in gold. Think long and hard about whether you have the time, skill and/or personality to be a good property manager. It just may be that hiring and outsourcing property management would enable you to have a better return on investment as well as keep you from being a burned out landlord.

Chapter 4: Creating the Right Mental Attitude

Like any other form of investing, you will need to have the right mental attitude when it comes to real estate investing as well.

Developing a positive belief mindset

As a real estate investor, if you experience positive feelings like joy, optimism, happiness and even love, you will open yourself up to being more profitable and can actually benefit from investing in real estate. If you have set yourself a goal of making $1000 per week, you will need to work towards achieving it. Once you get started, you will come across different investors with a positive mindset who have set higher goals for themselves. This will provide you with the necessary motivation and confidence to keep going.

Surround yourself with people who are positive and who have higher goals in life. Their enthusiasm and optimism are bound to rub off on you. If they can do it, so can you. You will learn that patience is a great virtue and by being patient you will be able to reap better profits. Don't be impatient and don't rush into something if you haven't thought it through. You needn't always make a big profit and quite frankly that's not possible at all times. It is okay to make small profits as well. This will keep you going. Hang around with positive people and this energy will definitely rub off on you.

You get what you think and expect

Positive thinking is quite a powerful tool. If you think positive thoughts, the outcome will be positive as well. Trust your gut and keep a positive mindset. If you firmly believe that your investment will do well, it will, provided the market conditions are favorable. Don't be too scared to take a calculated risk. All successful investors have a positive attitude about investing. Your thoughts are quite powerful; so, there is no point in investing in anything if you are always worried sick that it won't do well.

Ignoring and blocking out the naysayers

You don't necessarily have to follow what others say or do. A successful investor will often ignore what others have got to say and will do the opposite of what is perceived to be conventional. You are not truly free until you think for yourself. So, block out the negative noise and make your own decisions.

In real estate investing, it is okay to ignore conventional wisdom. You don't necessarily have to always invest in properties that are in nice parts of the town. You can also invest in distressed homes if you see that they have potential. If you want to, you can purchase properties at 20-30% under the market value and you can purchase them for cash as well. You needn't always invest with the thought of appreciation in your mind. Instead, you should be able to recognize the potential in a property, and buy it even if others fail to see this potential.

It is all about having a positive mindset and you will definitely make a handsome profit, it not immediately, eventually.

Chapter 5: Why Buying With Cash Lowers Risk

The crash in the housing market has managed to restructure the business of American mortgages. Part of this restructuring has resulted in stricter guidelines for obtaining mortgages, combined with an abundance of new properties for sale. This has, in turn, allowed some investors to buy properties for investment without using any leverage. This is a hot topic amongst real estate investors. Should you buy rental properties with all cash or should you mortgage until the wheels fall off. Like most things, there are pros and cons to both approaches. Let's take a closer look at these two options.

Property leveraging

There is and always has been a heated debate about whether property leveraging makes more sense when you are investing in properties. Some argue that you obtain a much greater return on your investment when you use leverage. The logic behind this argument is quite simple. If there is any appreciation in the value of the property, with a modest down payment, an investor will receive a higher return on their original capital invested.

Let's assume that you have made a down payment of 15% on a house valued at $500,000. The initial investment you will need to make would be $75,000. After ten years, this property has appreciated in value and the property is now valued at $650,000. In a case such as this, you can sell your investment and receive far more in proceeds than the initial investment of $75,000 you had made. In this case, you get your $75,000 principal investment back and also an additional $75,000 in the form of profit.

So, this would mean that you have risked much less than an investor who is buying with cash and also managed to earn yourself a good return. If you multiply this same formula over a few more properties, then you will make yourself quite a nice profit. A leveraged investor would have more opportunities coming his way than an investor buying with cash in these kinds of situations. A cash buyer will often buy a property by making use of liquid funds (money) that are available to them for making an investment. In comparison to this, a leveraged investor has the option of diversifying the way in which he can allocate money over multiple properties, and can, therefore, increase his return on investment in the long run. An example would be that if you had $100,000 worth of liquid capital, you could either buy one $100,000 property all cash or four $100,000 properties with four down payments of $25,000 using leverage. Yes, this is a simplistic example but the point is that leveraging enables an investor to spread their capital over multiple properties.

Risks of leveraging

Any given type of investment will have some inherent risks, especially when you are dealing with the uncertainties and fluctuations of a housing market. The most important one would be regarding the diversification of your money across multiple investments and this approach should only be taken into consideration by those investors who are well seasoned and thoroughly informed about the markets. You will need to have a strong grasp and understanding of the overall economic conditions, the health of the housing and property market, and also about the area in which you are considering buying a property. There are various advantages of taking out a loan for investing in a property. Be warned however, things might not work out as intended.

For instance, let us assume that each of the rental properties you own has depreciated quite steeply. In such a case, the leveraged investor would owe substantially more than what the investment is worth. Even one misstep can cost you a lot, especially if you have several different properties in your investment portfolio, all of which are leveraged. The bank advancing you the loan will be hit hard and you also stand the risk of damaging your credit score. The potential for a good return tends to attract a lot of investors to using debt for real estate investing. Indeed, some investors could not invest if they were not able to take advantage of using other people's money. However, you should be quite cautious when using debt for investment and should weigh all the risks that are involved. Using a levered strategy, you will also have to go through the entire mortgage process several times. The process of obtaining a mortgage is not always pleasant. This is another serious consideration for the investor.

Buying properties with cash

If you are interested in investing with cash, then you needn't have to worry about having to undergo the entire process of a mortgage application. You can make an investment quickly, provided there is an opportunity available. This is a major advantage over the levered strategy. The other benefit of being able to close a sale with cash is that you won't have to worry about interest payments either. Even if interest rates are low, paying interest can prove to be quite expensive in the long run and you don't have to worry about any of these things if you are investing with cash. If you have sufficient funds, then buying or investing in a property with cash definitely makes more sense if you believe that there will be favorable movement in the market in the coming years. Even without considering any appreciation, purchasing investment property with all cash can help you sleep well at night. If for some reason you have an extended vacancy, you can rest better knowing there is no bank or money lender breathing down your neck.

Let's assume that you have purchased a house for $400,000 in cash and you hold onto it until you see a favorable change in the market conditions. If you are right about the change in market conditions, and the value of the property appreciates to $500,000, this would mean that you have made a profit of $100,000, without having to worry about paying any interest to the bank on any mortgages. If you hold 100% equity in any given property, then it would also be easier for you to take out an equity loan against the property in the future, should the need arise. The all cash investment strategy will also enable you to earn a much larger cash flow than you would if the property were encumbered with debt.

Risks of investing with cash

On the flip side, it is quite a risky move to have all of your assets tied up in one investment.

Therefore, this approach might not be the best strategy available for an investor who has a limited sum of money for long-term usage. There can definitely be a positive increase in the value of a property. However, the property could also depreciate quite quickly as well. If this happens to be the case, then you will suffer a major setback. Diversification is one of the most important aspects of investing and tying up a major chunk of your assets in one kind of investment can result in a huge loss.

Both of these investment strategies, leverage and cash, have different advantages. However, the right choice for you will ultimately depend on your mindset. One thing that you should keep in your mind is that either of these strategies will require you to have a substantial amount of disposable income on hand. Even the leveraged buyers who will have spread out their investment across multiple properties will need to know that there is a certain risk of depreciation on all these properties and will need to keep a good sized reserve fund to cushion any blows.

Also remember, when you are purchasing a property with all cash, make sure that you aren't making use of your emergency funds or retirement funds for the acquisition. If an investor has large amounts of cash just lying around, the propensity for taking on risk would be the determining factor in such a case. A leveraged position investment will definitely offer a higher yield, but for those who don't want to get too involved and seek some equity and return on investment, then in such a case going the cash route might be a good option.

Chapter 6: Hiring Professional Property Managers to have Longevity in Real Estate Investing

If you are really serious about wanting to build a successful portfolio consisting of multiple rental properties, then you will need to take into consideration a really important aspect. Are you going to manage all of these properties on your own? If so, will you be able to? And should you hire a property manager who will help in handling these for you? This choice is quite a big decision since it has to do with how you spend your most valuable asset and that is time.

There really isn't a clear-cut answer to this dilemma. There are different reasons why choose to hire a property manager versus self-manage. I believe that the choice comes down to skill, personality and time. Do you have the time to devote to managing your properties or are you extremely busy with work and family obligations?

Can you be firm but fair or are you a little bit of a pushover? Are you knowledgeable about tenant law or knowledgeable about real estate in general? These considerations and more are major factors in the decision.

What is it that you are looking for from your rental properties? Regardless of your answer, the option that you select in this regard will have a huge impact on the success of your investment. So, it is essential that you get this right from the beginning. Take a minute and think about which of the following two categories you would fall under. The first one is where you want to create a job for yourself as the manager of your properties. And the second one is that you want to create a solid investment portfolio for yourself that will help you in earning passively. You should understand that you can't do both of these things simultaneously, since they work in opposite directions and lead to different experiences. If you want to become a property manager, then you will always have a "job" per se. If you want to retire early and enjoy the flow of passive income, then you most certainly cannot be the property manager.

Qualities of a good property manager

If you truly want to enjoy the freedom that passive income can give you, then you will need to hire someone who can take care of your properties for you. However, there are certain things that you will need to keep in your mind when hiring the services of a property manager. Not all property managers are good. It really isn't easy to find a good manager and you shouldn't take this process lightly. As the case would be with hiring the services of a professional like a lawyer or an accountant, there are certain property managers who are definitely worth their fee, and then there are some who just aren't worth considering. In fact, hiring a bad property manager can cost you thousands of dollars and turn a potentially profitable investment into a failed investment.

There are several factors that you should take into consideration before hiring a property manager. Listed below are some of these vital considerations.

- The property manager should know how to find good tenants and should also know

45

how to quickly get rid of undesirable tenants.

- They should have relationships with important vendors such as contractors, inspectors, and attorneys.

- They should be responsive, helpful and easy to communicate with.

- They should be well educated on the tenant laws in the state where the manage properties.

- They should have a good accounting system and are able to keep track of all income and expenses related to the management of your property.

Dealing with complaints from tenants

Who doesn't like the idea of earning passive income from renting out properties? But with the good also comes the bad. So, you will need to be ready to deal with all the problems and complaints that your tenants might have. By hiring the services of a property manager, you won't have to worry about this as much. Although you and your property manager are partners, and you will have input when problems arise, having a property manager keeps a buffer between you and your tenants.

Generally speaking, your property manager will handle most problems for you, with very little action from you. Your property manager would be responsible for taking care of issues like screening potential tenants, marketing and showing your property, and executing the lease agreement. Your property manager would also coordinate necessary repairs, late rent payments, move-out inspections and evictions, if necessary. Again, having a qualified and competent property management can make your real estate investment a very passive matter.

Focusing on your business

Take a look at any of the successful real estate moguls who have managed to amass huge wealth. How do you think managed to do all that? Surely, they would not have been able to achieve that level of success by personally tending to every complaint made by the tenant or by personally fixing the plumbing in each of their properties. They managed to reach a high level of success because they focused on the activities that they were good at and that also moved their business forward. They left the mundane, day to day operations to a highly competent manager. We should take note of this and strive to emulate this. Working on our business will move us to greater and greater heights than working in our business. Outsourcing has its place in real estate investing and we should take advantage of opportunities to outsource when they are available. This is especially true if the investor also has a full time job and/or a family. We cannot possible be all things to all people. We would stretch ourselves too thin and not find success in any area of our lives. Hiring a good property manager allows us to focus on our work and our business and still have time for family and friends. If you are serious about becoming a serious investor, you should think long and hard about if you would be able to manage your properties and grow your business or should you hand over the day to day management to someone else.

You cannot possibly be an expert at everything

You certainly cannot know everything. You might be good at a few things, but you probably cannot do the jobs of a handyman, a plumber, an electrician, a lawyer, an accountant, and other professionals. You are only human and it is okay if you do not have all of these skills or the time to perform all of these duties. Therefore, hiring a property manager who would have all the necessary contacts and relationships for taking care of the various problems that arise in real estate investing is critical. The property management company will provide you with every sort of professional service that you might need for the upkeep of your property and you certainly don't have to wreck your brain to figure things out by yourself. That's a huge burden lifted off your shoulders. This will save you time, energy, and money. You can also get more things done and you will definitely get better sleep at night knowing that your investments are in safe hands.

Invest anywhere

Most real estate investors tend to have certain self-imposed restrictions regarding investing in other markets. This isn't necessarily a bad thing, but you shouldn't hold your business back from growing because you are afraid to invest outside of your local market. Sometimes, the best investment opportunities are in a market far away from where you live. Also, sometimes it just doesn't make good financial sense to invest in your local market.

If you have hired a good property manager, then there is no real reason why you shouldn't invest outside of your local market. You don't have to physically drive to your property to have the property well managed. Your property manager will do all this for you.

Making the best investment decisions

A good property manager will always have your best interest in mind. Before you invest in a property, you can consult with your property manager to figure out whether a particular property would be a good investment or not. You can ask them different questions about the neighborhood you are interested in, the vacancy rates, the local market trends, the expected rent on the property, the costs of acquiring the property, getting the potential property thoroughly vetted and so on. Your property manager would be your personal consultant who will help you in making the best investment decisions.

Hiring a property manager is certainly a good idea. The services they provide usually outweigh the cost of hiring them. But be careful when hiring a property manager since the responsibility of taking care of your property would rest on them. You want someone who is capable of taking good care of your investment and who can also help further develop it. This will allow you to concentrate on the other things that require your attention. You can enjoy a steady flow of passive income without having to worry about different issues that crop up with the maintenance of investment properties. If you have multiple real estate investments, then a property manager would definitely be extremely helpful.

Chapter 7: Taking Action and Getting in the game

You will need to take the necessary actions for getting into the game of real estate investing. Reading and studying is good but nothing happens without action. In this chapter, you will learn about the different actions that you can take to help you getting started with real estate investing.

Saving for your first all cash purchase of rental property

The easiest manner in which you can make use of less cash for buying rental properties would be by choosing to invest in lower cost housing. The market prices are majorly responsible for determining the price of any rental property. With lower cost housing, you wouldn't have to spend all your money on acquiring a rental property. You can buy a property for a cheaper price and then renovate it if necessary.

You can also acquire rental property as an owner-occupant if you purchase a duplex, triplex or quad. In this case you would live in one unit and rent the other units out to others. This strategy would help you save a lot of cash. You could also make use of more favorable loan types such as FHA loans because you would be owner-occupying one unit.

Another method of reducing the amount of cash needed for purchasing a rental property is looking for seller financing. The one problem with seller financing is finding a seller who would be willing to give you the necessary credit. The cost of seller financing might be higher than your regular bank loan.

You could also partner with another investor. In this case, you would be investing less of your capital but still enjoying some of the profits that the investment shoots off. If you decide to invest with a partner, make sure you have an air-tight, written agreement. You don't to have any misunderstandings should something go wrong with the investment.

A more risky strategy is to buy a rental property by taking out a hard money loan and then refinancing that property into a traditional mortgage. With this strategy you will need to have a lot of experience because it is extremely risky. You would need to be prepared if you were not able to obtain a traditional mortgage. Plus, the interest rates on hard money loans are usually very high. This is to compensate the hard money lender for taking the risk of loaning you capital.

The most conservative manner in which you will be able to save money for investing would be by directly saving a portion of your income. You can save up to 50% of your personal income for the sake of investment. I realize that saving 50% of your income seems impossible but keep your mind open. Other people have done it, so why not you? With that said, I recognize that saving is not easy regardless of the amount of money you earn every month. Our society, as well as the economy, has been designed in such a manner that it is easy to spend and difficult to save money. If you manage to keep your spending habits under control, then you will be able to save more money. This doesn't mean that you shouldn't spend anything or that you should live frugally. It just means that you should go about spending your money in a very sensible manner.

Saving your tax refunds

You can always save up your tax refunds for making a future investment. It really isn't that difficult. You can set up your bank account in such a manner that the minute you receive the check for the tax refund, it is directly deposited in your savings account. This will help in making sure that you don't spend this amount on anything unnecessary. The more investment property you own, the bigger your tax refund might be. Therefore, as the years go by, it may be easier and easier to keep purchasing rental property simply by saving your tax refunds to use as down payments.

Setting aside a portion of your paycheck for investing

As mentioned earlier, you can simply save a portion of your monthly paycheck for investing. You can talk to your employer and get him to set aside a portion of your monthly paycheck for the purpose of investing. If you are self-employed, then you can direct your bank to set aside a portion of your monthly earnings for investing in real estate. They will simply need to withhold a certain percentage of your monthly income. Depending on your comfort level, you can decide this percentage. It can be as high or as low as you want it to be.

Living frugally

If you are really interested in making an investment in the real estate market, then you will certainly need a lot of funds. You can do this by living frugally for a while. Living frugally doesn't mean that you need to take on a Spartan existence. For a while, you can prioritize your expenses. Expenditures that seem unnecessary or ostentatious can be postponed for a while. Maybe you want to purchase a pair of Louis Vuitton pumps; this can certainly be put on hold for a while. You will be surprised with the amount of money you have been able to save by simply prioritizing your expenses. Whatever isn't a necessity can be certainly postponed.

Home Equity Lines on Primary Residence

There are different reasons for which you might want to get an HELOC (home equity line of credit) such as home renovations or even for investing in rental properties. Setting up an HELOC isn't expensive and it costs a fraction of the amount of credit that you are looking for. You might not need the money immediately; however, it does come in handy when a great investment opportunity comes along your way.

Qualifying for an HELOC

The qualifications that you will need to fulfill for getting an HELOC are quite similar to the ones that you will have to fulfill for getting a regular mortgage. The bank would require you to have a good credit score and an income that can help in backing up the amount for which you are seeking a loan. The requirements for all this would definitely differ from one bank to another and also on your loan requirements. You will need to have equity in the property you hold. Equity would be the difference in the value of your property and what you owe against that property. Banks have different ratios for loans and value and this will also depend on the type of property you are holding (whether it is an investment or a personal residence).

More Details on HELOCs

The variable rate on a home equity line of credit is around 2% above the Wall Street Journal - prime rate and the flooring rate is set at 5% while the ceiling rate is 21%. You wouldn't be charged any monthly or any yearly fees and will only have to pay interest on the money that you have actually made use of from the HELOC. The bank will need to get the property appraised and once that is done, after paying some fees, the HELOC will be granted. With this form of credit, you get the option of paying off the debt at any time that you like.

Most of the conventional banks offer HELOCs as well. However, it would be prudent to check the charges that are levied on such a line of credit. Make sure that you read and understand all the documents related to this financial product carefully before making a decision. Your property would be used as collateral and therefore is at stake.

Advantages of the HELOC

There are sometimes no closing costs. If you have a good credit score, then you may not have to pay any closing costs for setting up a HELOC. This means that you will not have to pay any application fees or the cost of an appraisal. With any form of standard equity loans, you would have to pay these costs.

No fees for cash withdrawals

When you withdraw an advance on your credit card, there is a fee that is levied by the bank. This is called a cash advance. However, with a HELOC you would not have to pay a fee for withdrawing any funds. If the lender levies a fee on every cash withdrawal, then you should certainly look somewhere else.

Low rates of interest

The rates of interest charged on HELOCs are quite low. Since this is a form of home equity, the rates on this are low when compared to various other unsecured loans like personal loans or the interest levied on credit cards. The rates of HELOCs can fluctuate over a period of time since they are loans of an adjustable rate. According to law, HELOCs are supposed to have a limit on the maximum rate of interest that can be charged during the duration of the loan.

Conversion

Most of the HELOCs tend to have a provision for converting these to a fixed-rate loan if you want to have a fixed interest rate on the payments. When the repayment phase starts, this tends to happen automatically.

You can pay it off whenever you like

You will be able to pay off the balance of the HELOC whenever you like. There aren't any fees levied for early repayment of the loan. However, there are certain HELOCs that will charge you a fixed fee if you haven't maintained a particular minimum balance of funds in a given year.

Tax benefits

Since this is a form of mortgage, the interest that you pay on the HELOC is deductible. Most HELOC users would have a certain plan in mind for justifying the use of funds. However, this isn't necessary. Once the line of credit has been set up, you can pretty much use it as you please without having to inform the lender of its use. However, usually a lender will ask about the intended use of the funds during the application process.

Disadvantages of HELOCs

Low payment option

You can repay the HELOC, as you like during the lifetime of the loan. This means that you can simply pay the interest every month and leave the principal payments for a while. However, if this is the strategy you follow, then it will be a long time before you are able to fully repay the principal.

Rise in the interest rate

HELOCs do sometimes start out with low rates of interest. However, the rates of interest can increase if inflation sets in. This can catch the investor completely by surprise. This wouldn't be the case with any fixed interest loan.

Using your home for borrowing

Make sure that the reason for which you are borrowing is worth it. Since you are literally using your home as your personal piggy bank, your home wouldn't be free of encumbrances until the last penny has been repaid.

Payments

By the time you have reached the end of the draw period of an HELOC, you will need to start repaying the principal along with the interest. This means that your monthly payments will increase and it can come as quite a rude shock for the borrower. From having to pay only a couple of dollars to paying a couple of hundred dollars every month is not a pleasant experience. So, don't give into the temptation of borrowing more than you had initially planned. This coupled with a rise in the interest rates would be a terrible blow to the borrower.

Losing home value

Another major risk of a HELOC is that the property you have borrowed against can depreciate in value. This would be quite a big problem if you were counting on reselling the house or for refinancing against it to cover the equity loan. At times, it even happens that the value of the mortgage and the HELOC together would be more than the actual worth of the house. As a rule of thumb, you should never borrow more than 80% of the market value of your house. The buffer of 20% will provide you the necessary cushioning in case of the market crashes. In most cases, lenders will have a cap on the loan to value (LTV) that they will enable you to borrow against.

Side jobs/businesses for extra cash that can be used towards purchasing rental property

You can start your own business. When you have a business of your own, then you have got all the control and the opportunity for making more money that can be used as capital for real estate investing. Holding and maintaining rental properties could be a business as well. You will simply need to make sure that you are running the business and it isn't the other way around. The business should be able to make money for you without much hassle.

Asking for a raise or making a career change

The easiest manner in which you can get more money is by simply asking for it. If you are working for someone else and you know that you are doing a good job, you can simply ask for a raise. If you think you haven't got any reason for asking for a raise, then in such a case work harder so that you can ask for what you deserve. If you think that you have reached a saturation point in your current employment, then you can consider changing your career. You can shift to doing work that you genuinely enjoy and like doing. It is never too late to do something you love. There are many different ways in which you can make more money for yourself by doing something you love.

Chapter 8: Learn From your Past Failures and Don't Let Them Stop You

Getting back to investing

Numerous people have made nice profits by investing in real estate. But, it is not as easy as it looks. It is a business that takes time to grow and this is where most investors fail. Some investors want to be financially free immediately. If you are not starting with a ton of capital to invest, immediate financial freedom is not likely. This is not the kind of business where you can expect to get rich quickly. It takes patience and perseverance to succeed in real estate investing.

What to do if you encounter a failure

The only way to get over your failures is to not let them discourage you. Start fresh with a new vision. Make an analysis of all the mistakes you made and figure out solutions so that you will be prepared next time. Overcome your failure by being more careful the next time. Make a plan to better yourself in this field. When a deal looks too good to be true, it usually is! So, it's better to do your groundwork and due diligence before you make an investment. Start investing in real estate as a side business while still holding down a steady job, so you can minimize the financial risk of investing.

Starting a real estate investing business can be really hard because you might not have the willingness to take the necessary risks that lead to success. The fear of failure and the pressure to succeed can be paralyzing. Like the first day of school, your first deal will be grueling and laborious. So many real estate investors attend too many seminars, read too many books and spend too much time analyzing rather than taking action. This is sometimes called analysis paralysis.

A lot of dedication, determination and endurance are required to make it in this business. Be responsible and make an investment in your education first. Attending a few seminars to get a gist about the business is a good idea, to begin with. Reading a few books to get a definite clarity about the different concepts related to real estate investing should also be done. But, during the initial stages of operation, it would be wise to get a consultant or mentor who will be able to guide you and provide valuable insight for your benefit.

It is inevitable that mistakes will happen; you will get flustered and consider quitting. Remember that many real estate investors have been through this and were able to overcome the hurdles to become successful. So, don't lose hope and find an experienced person to help you out and find viable solutions to your problems. Eventually, success will come to you with open arms.

Seek competent guidance from qualified real estate agents

When there is an economic strain, everyone wants to make responsible choices about where they spend their money. When purchasing real estate, every penny matters. Everyone has certain criterion when it comes to buying real estate. Some people want a big house with a swimming pool while some prefer a cozy apartment or loft. However, purchasing real estate for investment is different than buying a personal residence. It helps if you can find a real estate agent who either is an investor himself or who works extensively with real estate investors. The difference in skill necessary for buying investment property can be astounding. There are some agents out there who don't know there is any difference and will lead you astray because they don't fully understand real estate investments.

Benefits of seeking advice from real estate agents

They have the right educational background

Real estate agents have the correct knowledge about making and breaking deals. They know the right procedures and formalities that are necessary for buying and selling properties. They can also give you the necessary details and suggest the right properties based on your prerequisites. They also have knowledge about the local, state, national and international market so they can guide you smoothly.

Good network and connections

Real estate agents who have been in the market long enough have reliable connections that can provide them the right information. They have connections in the local market as well and know the right places that are available for sale. They will definitely help you to make a profitable decision for your business. They have professional partnerships and contacts in the market and can equip you with a compiled list of references that they have worked with before.

Help in paperwork

This is a big one. We all know how exhausting the paperwork is when a property has to be sold or bought. Real estate agents have been through this process many times and can help you avoid errors in the paperwork, which will save you a lot of time, trouble and money in the future.

Valuable negotiation skills

Real estate agents can help you to effectively negotiate the prices and terms with the other party on your behalf. This saves you from trouble and unnecessary tension. These brokers have exceptional negotiating and mediating skills. They can marvelously handle situations with a sound mind and this will prove very beneficial to you.

Price counseling

Real estate agents are very experienced and know the value of the land or property and can make sure that you don't get ripped off and pay the right price. They can help you find the perfect fit for your budget.

Hiring a real estate agent can give you the right idea of what you're in for and give you an inside peek on how the real estate business works too.

There are some reputable turnkey real estate providers who can help you invest out of state. Some pundits say that it is better to invest in local markets so you can check up on your properties from time to time and inspect them. Many real estate agents encourage their clients to buy properties that are closer to where they live for ease and convenience. Yet, out of state turnkey properties can be very profitable investments and this market is still untapped due to the majority of investors focusing on their local markets.

There are a few things that need to considered when you plan to invest in an out of state market such as -

- State laws
- Market trends
- Price to rent ratios

There are many other items that could be added to this non-exhaustive list, but if these three items are satisfied, then you can move on to the next step.

Turnkey real estate companies usually buy properties or homes off market from wholesalers or directly from distressed sellers, rehab and renovate the properties and then sell the properties to other investors. These turnkey properties require less effort from the buyer investor and are almost always already rented out which saves time. These turnkey real estate providers usually also offer property management services to the investor. Investing with turnkey providers can be a whole book by itself. Turnkey investing looks easy but buyer beware still applies. There are many horror stories on the internet from investors who have been burned badly by investing out of state with non-reputable turnkey providers. Due diligence is extremely important if you are considering investing via the turnkey route.

Benefits of out of state turnkey investments

It is obviously considered a better option to buy properties that are closer to where you live so that you are just a drive away so you can check up on them, but there is a lot of time and money involved in getting these properties ready to rent. But turnkey properties that have already been given a makeover and have renters in waiting or have already been rented out can be a very convenient option for investors. It will save them a lot of time that is loss in rehabbing the property, marketing the property and securing tenants. The revenue, in this case, will start flowing sooner.

Conclusion

I would like to thank you once again for purchasing this book and I hope that it was an informative read.

Real estate investing isn't that difficult once you realize what you need to do. Armed with all the information that has been provided in this book, you have the basic tools needed to make a smart investment. As with any other investment, there are certain risks to be considered. If you are aware of these risks, then you can take the necessary steps to reduce these risks.

Keep a positive mindset. Don't think of minor setbacks as failures. Just keep moving forward. With a strong "reason why" you can begin real estate investing by devising a good plan, preparing for contingencies, and raising the necessary startup capital. Remember, you can always seek professional help to gain information that you need to fill in your knowledge gaps.

All that is left now is for you to take action. Be

patient, stay positive, and do your due diligence. Success is waiting for you.

I wish you all the best!